What's Great?

by John Stafford
illustrations by Marilyn Mets

H a r c o u r t   B r a c e   &   C o m p a n y

Orlando Atlanta Austin Boston San Francisco Chicago Dallas New York Toronto London

What's great?
Daybreak is great!

What's great?
Steak is great!

What's great?
A sleigh is great!

What's great?
A neigh is great!

What's great?
Getting weighed is great!

What's great?
Eight kittens are great!

What's great?
Freight trains are great!

Daybreak, steak, sleighs,
neighs, getting weighed,
eight kittens, freight
trains—they are all great!

But I know someone
who is VERY great.

I have a great name
for her.

Mom the Great!